About this book

The beginning of this book shows you different herbs which you can grow in pots indoors, in window boxes, in containers outdoors and in various garden plans. It explains how to care for every herb pictured. The last part of the book gives step-by-step directions on how to grow and care for your herbs and ways to use them once they are fully grown. There is even a chart that gives all the information about each plant. Latin names are included, as well as common names, so you can find all the plants you want in catalogues or in garden centers.

Remember that part of the fun of growing plants is being able to share them with other people. You will have herbs to give away as well as herbal presents that you make with them.

Designer : Pat Butterworth
Cover illustration by Barbara Firth
Additional illustrations :
Jane Wolsak pages 4, 5, 37

© Walker Books Limited 1980
First published by Walker Books,
London, England

LIBRARY OF CONGRESS CATALOG CARD NO. 80-82106
First American edition

Printed and bound in Italy by
Il Resto del Carlino, Bologna

ISBN 0-316-89974-7

Contents

The Herb Growing Book

Written
by Rosemary Verey
Feature illustrations
by Barbara Firth
Activity illustrations
by Elizabeth Wood

LITTLE, BROWN AND CO.

Boston

How to use this book

Symbols
You will see symbols used on the step-by-step pages in this book. The symbols show you the kind of light plants need, when to feed them, when to water them and if they need a hot or cool place.

Indirect light This means light that is not full sunlight.

Direct light Some seeds, plants or seedlings need to grow in direct light.

Watering This shows you when to water your plants.

Light watering This means to use a fine-rose on your watering can.

Annual An annual is grown from seed. It flowers and dies in one year A hardy annual won't be hurt by frost. A half-hardy annual shouldn't be planted outdoors until all danger of frost has passed.

Seed leaves The small round leaves on a seedling. They are a different shape from the leaves that grow as the plant gets bigger.

Biennial A plant that grows leaves the first year. It flowers, grows seeds and then dies the next year.

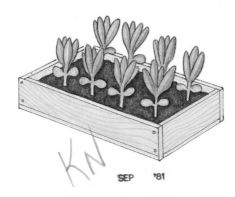

Perennial This takes two years to flower but then flowers year after year. It dies down in the winter and sends up new shoots the next spring. A half-hardy perennial can live through a winter indoors, or outdoors if it's a mild winter.

Rosette A cluster of leaves usually at ground level, growing from a central point.

SEP '81

Hot, dark place Some seedlings need to start growing in these conditions.

Cool, dark place Some plants need these conditions.

Names
All plants have Latin names which botanists (plant scientists) use. If you want to know the Latin names for the plants in this book, look in the Index on p. 40. If a plant also has a common English name, it is the name you'll see used on all the other pages.

Hardening off This is getting plants slowly used to a cooler temperature so you can plant them outdoors. For one week, put them outdoors in a sheltered place during the day and bring them indoors at night. Then you can plant them outdoors.

Be sure that:
1. you always clean up after doing a project.
2. you **ask an adult** to help you, wherever it's written in this book.

Shrub A plant that has branches and woody stems.

Variegated Leaves that have markings of deeper and lighter colors on them.

Hardwood A stem which has been growing from spring until autumn, or longer. Take hardwood cuttings in autumn.

Bulb An underground storage organ which has separate, fleshy scales. Tiny bulbs are called bulbils. Chives have these.

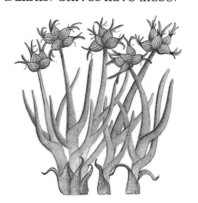

Softwood A new young growth on a plant. Take softwood cuttings in the spring and early summer.

Node A point on a stem from which a leaf or a new stem will grow.

Uses of herbs

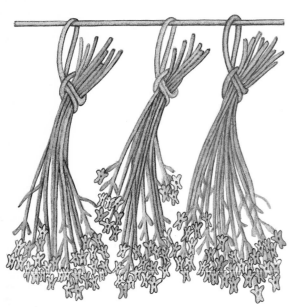

You can grow herbs indoors on a sunny windowsill in many kinds of containers. Old cans are good to use if you paint them with enamel and **ask an adult** to punch drainage holes in the bottoms. You can also use dishes and plastic food containers. Put down gravel at the bottom if a container doesn't have drainage holes. Once your herbs are grown, use them to flavor foods, and to make pomanders, nosegays, lavender bags and pot-pourri (see pp. 28-34).

You can also grow herbs outdoors. If you don't have a piece of ground or a garden, plant herbs and cuttings that you have grown indoors in tubs, pots or barrels (see p. 21). The plant chart tells you which plants are good to grow in containers (see p. 39). Some herbs can grow outdoors all year round. No matter where you grow herbs, you can use them to make things and in cooking.

Indoors and outdoors

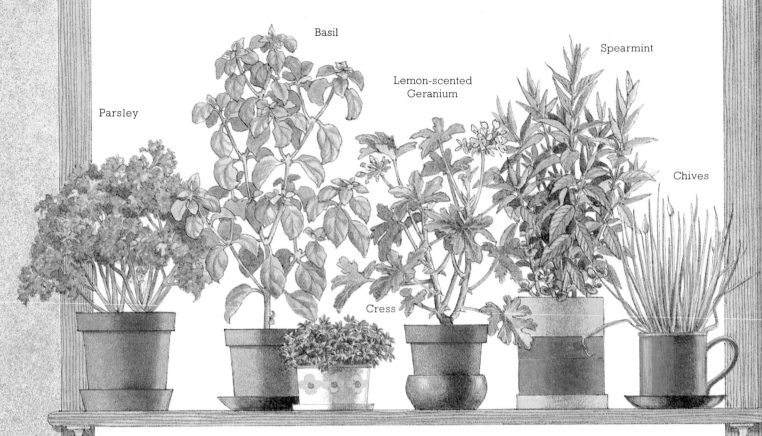

Parsley

Basil

Lemon-scented
Geranium

Spearmint

Chives

Cress

You can grow herbs in pots or cans on a sunny window sill indoors. Paint the cans with enamel first and **ask an adult** to punch drainage holes in the bottoms. Fill the cans in the same way as you do pots (see p. 27).

Parsley and Basil are annuals. Sow seeds into trays and then prick them out (see pp. 22-23) or sow them straight into pots. Three plants will fit in a 12.75cm-wide pot.

Mint is a perennial. Ask a gardener friend to give you a root of mint. Plant this in a pot. Lay it flat and cover it with 2cm of potting compost. Cut off the shoots when they are about 30cm long so new ones will grow.

Chives are perennial. Grow them from seeds (see p. 22) or ask friends who have a clump growing if they will give you some bulbs. Plant each tiny bulb 2cm apart. They spread to fill their container. Cut off the leaves when they are 7 to 10cm long. New leaves will grow.

You can buy a Lemon-scented Geranium and take softwood cuttings from it (see p. 24). It grows well indoors. Use the scented leaves for pot-pourri (see p. 32).

Grow Cress at any time of year in a pot or shallow dish. Half-fill it with compost or line it with blotting paper or flannel. Water this well, then sow seeds thickly and evenly. Cut Cress when it is 5cm high to use in salad.

If you don't have space for an herb garden you can still enjoy growing herbs in containers outdoors. Choose a place where there is enough room for large pots. Plastic pots are inexpensive and less likely to break than clay. A barrel cut in half is also very good. You can put a small can on top of a larger one, too, after the larger one has been filled with compost. Be sure that you have space for the size of container you want before you buy it.

A very nice herb to keep in a pot is a Bay tree. It is evergreen and lives for a long time. Clip back the new branches to one half their length in spring and autumn to keep the tree tidy. You can shape it into a ball if you wish. You can take hardwood cuttings (see p. 26) in autumn, but you may find them more difficult to root than some other cuttings.

Surround your Bay tree with Thyme, a perennial, and Parsley, grown as an annual. Grow these from seed sown directly into the pot or sow them in a tray indoors (see p. 22) and plant them out into the pot when they are large enough to handle (see p. 23).

You can also grow Thyme and Basil in a tub on their own.

Bay tree

Basil

Lemon Verbena

Thyme   Parsley   Lemon Thyme   Apple Mint

If your windowsill is wide enough and gets enough sun, you can grow herbs in pots and window boxes.

A box can be wooden or plastic. It should be at least 20cm deep. Be sure that it sits firmly on the sill and can't slide off. Remember to put a tray underneath if the box has drainage holes, so that water can't drip down on anything below. Fill your window box on the sill, because it will be too heavy to lift afterwards (see p. 27).

You can sow all the seeds indoors (see p. 22) and then plant herbs in a window box or pots in late spring, when there is no danger of frost.

Thyme, Chives, Marjoram and Winter Savory are perennials. Sage and Rosemary are perennial shrubs. Basil and trailing Nasturtiums are annuals. Parsley is a biennial but should be grown as an annual.

Before you put herbs into a box, stand them, still in their pots, where you want them to grow. You will be able to see if you like the arrangement. Then take the plants out of their pots (see p. 25).

Rosemary

Basil

Parsley   Chives   Golden Lemon Thyme   Wild Thyme

If you put all your herbs into one box, plant your taller herbs first. Don't put in too many, or they will stop light reaching inside. Shrubs such as Rosemary and Gray- or Purple-leafed Sage can be clipped into tidy shapes. Next, put Thyme, Marjoram and Winter Savory towards the front of your box (the front is the long side furthest away from your window). Allow enough space between each of these plants and just behind them for Parsley, two or three clumps of Chives and some Sweet Basil.

If you wish, you can sow seeds of trailing Nasturtiums along the very front of the box in late spring. When these grow, they will hang down over the edge of the box.

You can also put cuttings (see pp. 24-26) of some of your herbs in a window box or in pots.

Use a watering can with a long spout to water your plants. Remember to give them enough water if the sun is very strong in summer. It's best to water early in the morning or late in the afternoon.

Tri-color Sage

Marjoram

Basil

Winter Savory

Nasturtium

All these plants are annuals (see p. 2).

Marigolds will brighten up your herb bed. They grow up to 38cm. Sow the seeds straight into the ground in spring (see p. 20). Thin them out to 25cm apart (see p. 37). You can also grow them in 12cm pots filled with potting compost (see p. 22). Thin these to three seedlings in each pot. Use a few petals in a salad, or dry them for a pot-pourri (see p. 32).

Grow Basil the same way as Marigolds. It grows up to 30cm. You can use the leaves in a tomato and bean salad or in soups and omelettes.

Grow Summer Savory the same way as Marigolds, too. It grows up to 25cm. Add the leaves to soups or fish. Chop up the leaves and flowers to sprinkle on cheese dishes. Try them with melted butter on broad beans.

Parsley is an herb with many uses. It is pretty as an edge to a bed or growing at the center of a bed. It decorates any dish and the flavor is delicious. As well as being tasty, it has iron and vitamins. You can sow it in pots indoors (see p. 22) or straight into the ground (see p. 20). It grows to 38cm.

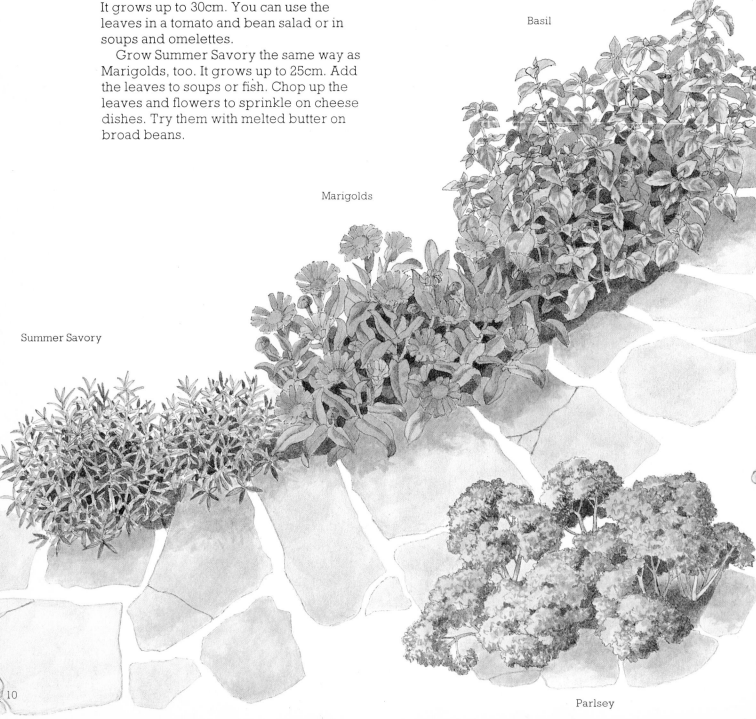

Basil

Marigolds

Summer Savory

Parlsey

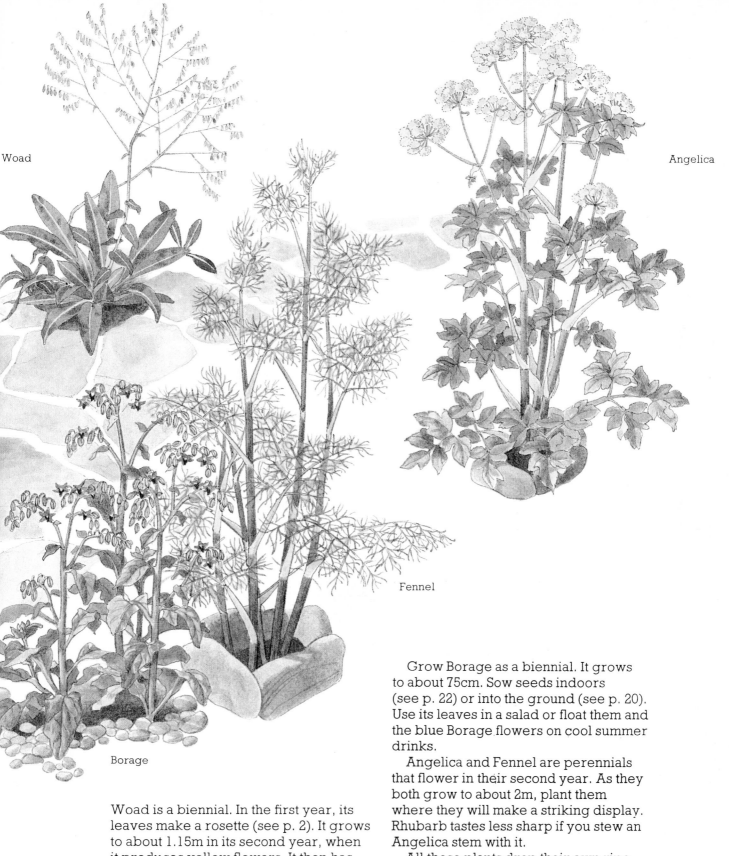

Woad

Angelica

Fennel

Borage

Woad is a biennial. In the first year, its leaves make a rosette (see p. 2). It grows to about 1.15m in its second year, when it produces yellow flowers. It then has black seeds which you can use in dried flower arrangements.

Grow Borage as a biennial. It grows to about 75cm. Sow seeds indoors (see p. 22) or into the ground (see p. 20). Use its leaves in a salad or float them and the blue Borage flowers on cool summer drinks.

Angelica and Fennel are perennials that flower in their second year. As they both grow to about 2m, plant them where they will make a striking display. Rhubarb tastes less sharp if you stew an Angelica stem with it.

All these plants drop their own ripe seeds into the ground where new plants will then grow.

Caraway can grow to 50cm. Gather seeds from full-grown plants by cutting off the seed heads when they turn brown. It is best to sow seeds as soon as they are ripe in the autumn. Seeds sown in spring take a long time to start growing. Sow seeds outdoors (see p. 20) in a sunny place. Thin them out to 20cm apart (see p. 37). If you want to use seeds to add a licorice-like flavor to cakes, biscuits and bread, **ask an adult** to scald them first in boiling water. Then dry them in the sun and store them in an airtight jar.

French Sorrel grows to 30cm in a sunny place. Grow it from seeds outdoors (see p. 20) or by root division (see p. 26). Use a few Sorrel leaves in soup. They taste bitter, so don't add too many.

Goose Foot grows to 75cm. Sow seeds in a shady place outdoors in spring (see p. 20). Thin seedlings to 25cm apart. Divide plants when they are two years old. You can cook and eat the leaves of this herb in summer.

Sow Anise seeds outdoors in a sunny place in spring. Thin seedlings to 25cm apart. When their seeds are ripe, shake them off the stems into a bag. Store in a closed jar until you need them to flavor sweets or cakes.

Rosemary

Goose Foot

Caraway

Sorrel

Anise

12

Sage can be gray, purple, or tri-colored (gray, purple and white). Use Gray Sage to flavor pork. Purple and Tri-color Sages will help your garden look pretty. Grow Sage from seeds (see p. 20) or softwood cuttings in spring (see p. 24). They root easily.

Grow French Tarragon in a sunny, well-drained place (see p. 20), so it will be hardy (see p. 2). Use it when cooking chicken or fish. Grow new plants by root division (see p. 26).

Chives can edge a path. If you keep cutting them just above the tiny bulbs (see p. 3), which you do not eat, they send up new leaves. Chop them into soups, salad, eggs or cream cheese.

Garlic will grow to about 25 to 45cm in a sunny place. Nip off the white flowers as they grow, or the flavor of the cloves will be ruined. Grow Garlic from cloves planted in the spring or the autumn.

Grow Rosemary in a sunny place with good drainage. You can train it to grow against a wall. It will also make a hedge about 1m high. Take hardwood cuttings in autumn (see p. 26). Plant them in a pot (see p. 27) or in the ground (see p. 20). They root easily.

Gray Sage

French Tarragon

Garlic

Chives

All these plants are small shrubs (see p.3).

If you grow Lemon Verbena in a warm, sheltered place with good drainage, it can survive a few degrees of frost. Very harsh frost will kill its top growth, but it will shoot again from the ground in spring. If your plant is young, dig it up and put it in a pot indoors for the winter (see p. 27). When the leaves drop, water very little until spring. Then cut its branchlets and water regularly. Plant it outdoors again in late spring (see p. 21). The leaves have a nice scent. You can grow Lemon Verbena from softwood cuttings in May (see p. 24).

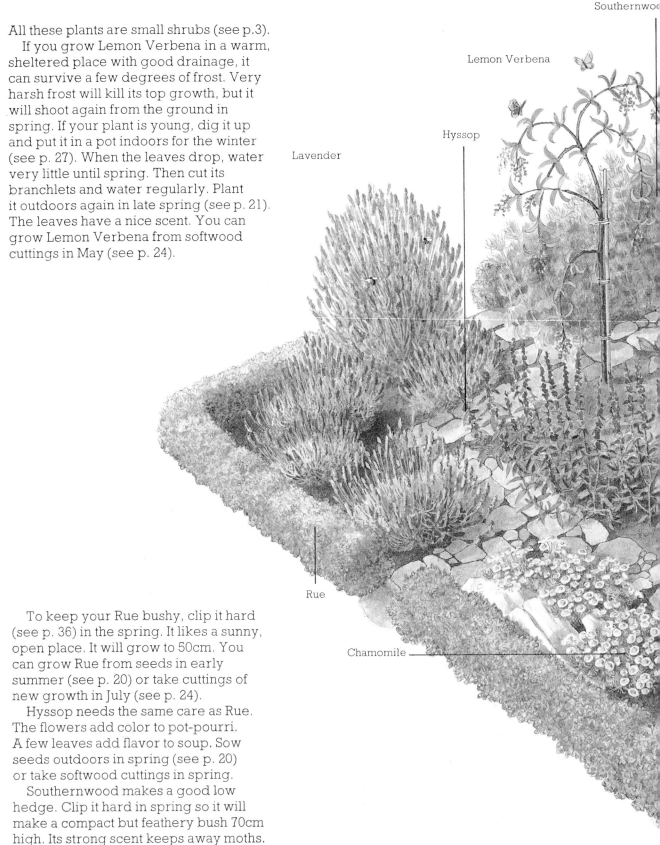

Southernwood

Lemon Verbena

Hyssop

Lavender

Rue

Chamomile

To keep your Rue bushy, clip it hard (see p. 36) in the spring. It likes a sunny, open place. It will grow to 50cm. You can grow Rue from seeds in early summer (see p. 20) or take cuttings of new growth in July (see p. 24).

Hyssop needs the same care as Rue. The flowers add color to pot-pourri. A few leaves add flavor to soup. Sow seeds outdoors in spring (see p. 20) or take softwood cuttings in spring.

Southernwood makes a good low hedge. Clip it hard in spring so it will make a compact but feathery bush 70cm high. Its strong scent keeps away moths. Grow it from hardwood cuttings, using the pieces you cut off in spring.

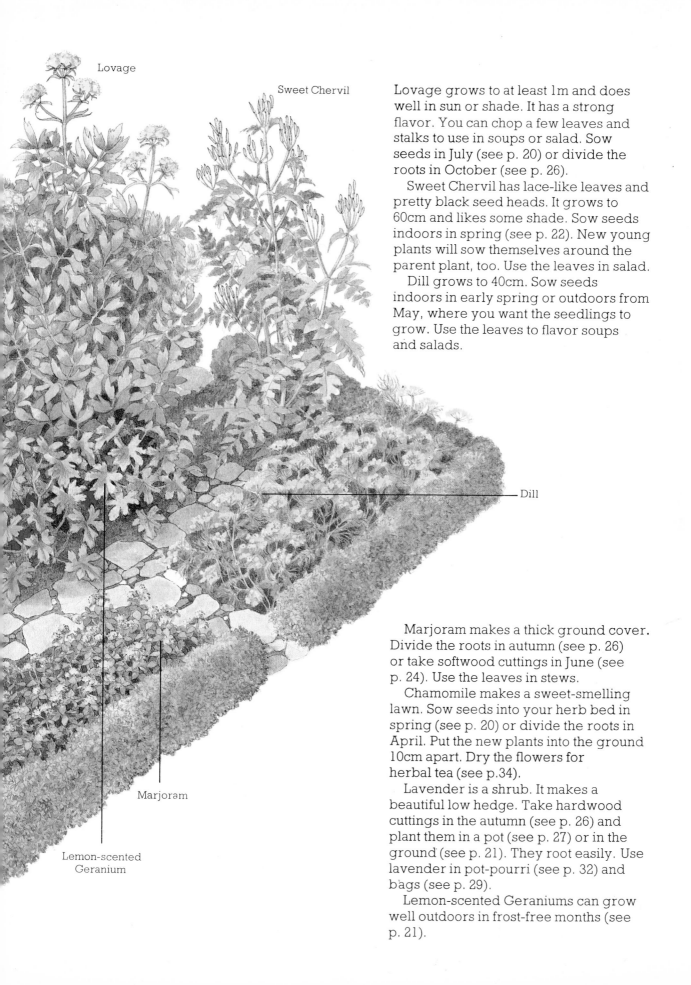

Lovage

Sweet Chervil

Dill

Marjoram

Lemon-scented Geranium

Lovage grows to at least 1m and does well in sun or shade. It has a strong flavor. You can chop a few leaves and stalks to use in soups or salad. Sow seeds in July (see p. 20) or divide the roots in October (see p. 26).

Sweet Chervil has lace-like leaves and pretty black seed heads. It grows to 60cm and likes some shade. Sow seeds indoors in spring (see p. 22). New young plants will sow themselves around the parent plant, too. Use the leaves in salad.

Dill grows to 40cm. Sow seeds indoors in early spring or outdoors from May, where you want the seedlings to grow. Use the leaves to flavor soups and salads.

Marjoram makes a thick ground cover. Divide the roots in autumn (see p. 26) or take softwood cuttings in June (see p. 24). Use the leaves in stews.

Chamomile makes a sweet-smelling lawn. Sow seeds into your herb bed in spring (see p. 20) or divide the roots in April. Put the new plants into the ground 10cm apart. Dry the flowers for herbal tea (see p.34).

Lavender is a shrub. It makes a beautiful low hedge. Take hardwood cuttings in the autumn (see p. 26) and plant them in a pot (see p. 27) or in the ground (see p. 21). They root easily. Use lavender in pot-pourri (see p. 32) and bags (see p. 29).

Lemon-scented Geraniums can grow well outdoors in frost-free months (see p. 21).

Mint, Bergamot, Lemon Balm and Tree Onion are all perennials (see p. 2).

Plant Mint in an old bottomless bucket sunk into the ground to stop the plant spreading quickly. Grow new plants by dividing the roots (see p. 26).

There are several varieties of Mint. Dry the leaves of Ginger Mint and Eau de Cologne Mint, which both grow to 30cm, for pot-pourri (see p. 32).

Variegated Apple Mint, which grows to 30cm, is pretty in an herb bed.

Spearmint and Apple Mint, which grow to 1m, are the best for cooking, and making mint sauce.

Lemon Balm leaves make delicious herbal tea (see p. 34). Divide the roots for new plants.

Bergamot, or Bee Balm, has pretty, shaggy, red flowers on square, 66cm-high stems. Shred the sweet-smelling fresh leaves into a salad, or use them for herbal tea. Dry them for a pot-pourri. Buy plants and put them in your herb bed (see p. 21). Divide the roots in autumn to propagate.

A Tree Onion is fun to have in your herb bed. One onion bulb will grow new bulbs all around it during the summer. The onion stems grow to 40cm, then grow a cluster of tiny bulbs on top. Cut these off for flavoring food, or plant them just on top of the soil to make more Tree Onions.

Eau de Cologne Mint

Ginger Mint

Variegated Apple Mint

Spearmint

Santolina is a gray shrub with strong-smelling leaves. Keep it in a tidy shape by clipping it just above the old wood in April (see p. 36). New shoots will soon grow. If you don't clip it this way, it will become leggy after two years. Dry the leaves for your pot-pourri (see p. 32). Buy plants and put them in your herb bed (see p. 21). To propagate Santolina take hardwood cuttings in spring or in autumn (see p. 26).

There are many varieties of Thyme. The one which makes a thick carpet on the ground is *Thymus serpyllum*. In midsummer, it is covered with pink, mauve or brilliant crimson flowers, which attract bees.

There is Golden Thyme, Lemon Thyme with green leaves and Lemon Thyme with silver or golden variegated leaves. These all grow into solid clumps about 20cm high.

Wild Thyme from Provence in France has sweet-smelling, gray leaves. You can grow new plants from cuttings. Look underneath all your Thyme plants for pieces that have taken root. **Ask an adult** to cut them off. Plant them (see p. 21) or give them away.

Tree Onion

Bergamont

Balm

Wild Thyme

Santolina

Planning your garden

It will help if you make a plan of your herb garden before you sow seeds or put plants in the ground. You can decide on the pattern that you want and see if there is enough space for your plants to grow. Remember that Lavender, Southernwood, Rosemary and Rue all make good low hedges.

You will need
Pencil
Ruler
Sheet of white paper
String
Sticks
Pebbles or stones for paths, or hedges of herbs

1. Using the pencil and ruler, draw lines at equal spaces across the paper.

2. Draw lines down the paper. They should be the same distance apart as the lines going across, so that you have squares. Each square equals 30cm of your garden.

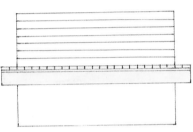
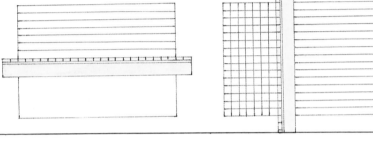

3. Draw your garden plan on to the squared paper. Leave about the same amount of space for each herb patch as shown on p. 21. Label the herbs you want in each space.

4. Prepare your ground outdoors (see pp. 20–21). Now you are ready to transfer your plan to the ground.

5. Use string to measure the lengths of the borders. Each length should be the same size as the scale you worked out on your paper.

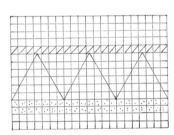
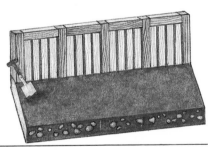
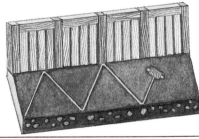

6. Push sticks into the ground to mark the top and bottom of each herb patch. Tie the string to the sticks.

7. The lines of string mark the area for each herb patch. Put down pebbles or stones or plant hedges of herbs (see p. 20) along the lines. These mark your patches.

8. Now plant whichever herbs you choose within each patch (see p. 20).

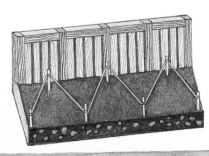
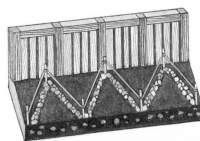
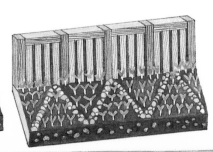

The plan on the top of this page is drawn on paper ten squares across and ten squares down. The plan is square-shaped, but you can turn it to make it into a diamond shape like the one on p. 14. The brown areas shown here are for paths and the green areas are for bordering hedges. Plant your herbs in the blank areas.

The plan on the bottom is also drawn on paper ten squares across and ten squares down. It is like the garden shown on p. 12. The paths and herbs on this plan are shown already in place. To make a circular shape in your garden, put a stick into the ground. Tie one end of a string to the stick. If you want your circle to be 60cm across, the string should be 30cm long. You can make the string as long as you want, for smaller or larger circles. Hold the loose end of string and walk as far away from the stick as you can. Now walk around in a circle, keeping the string tightly stretched. As you walk, 'draw' on the ground by letting sand trickle from a bottle in your other hand.

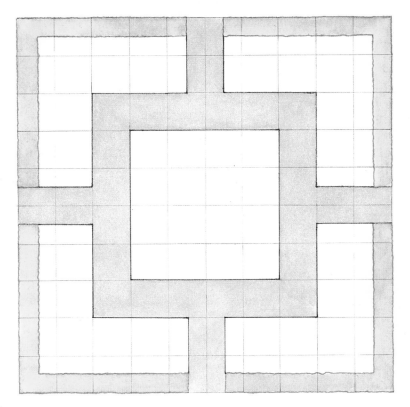

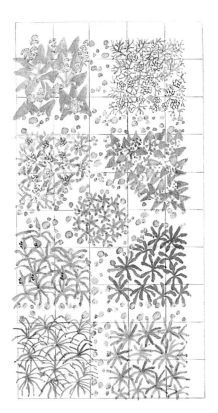

Sowing seeds outdoors

The ground must be carefully prepared before sowing seeds or planting herbs. You can sow seeds into a special seed bed and transplant seedlings later to an herb bed, or sow seeds directly into an herb bed. A seed bed must be sheltered and get a lot of direct sun.

You will need
Spade
Bucket for weeds and roots
Leaf mold, manure or organic matter (see p. 36)
Garden fork
Rake
Watering can
2 sticks and string
Seed packets from a garden center

1. In the autumn, turn over the ground with a fork. Take out weeds and perennial roots for your compost heap (see p. 36).

2. Dig in some leaf mold, manure or organic matter from your compost heap (see p. 36).

3. In the spring, dig the ground again lightly with a fork. Take out any new weeds and any large stones.

4. Rake the ground until it is level and the soil on top is fine.

5. Tread over the soil making it firm. Do this when the ground is dry so the soil won't stick to your boots.

6. Rake again so that the soil will be very fine. If the ground is very dry, water it well and wait a day.

7. If this is a seed bed, make shallow straight rows (called 'drills') about 20cm apart with the edge of the rake.

8. Sow the seeds. Tap the seed packet gently over the drills or tip the seeds into your palm and sow them with your other hand.

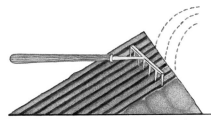

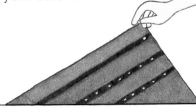

9. If this is an herb bed, sow the seeds evenly and thinly over the ground, not into drills.

10. Rake lightly across the seeds, covering them with a very thin layer of soil. Water when the ground is dry.

11. When the seedlings grow, thin them out to 10cm apart for a seed bed and about 22cm apart for an herb bed (see p. 37).

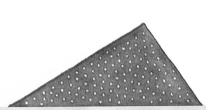

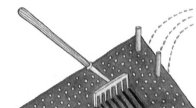

Planting out

Plant bought herbs and rooted cuttings straight into an herb bed. If possible, prepare your ground in the autumn so the winter frost will break down the soil. Otherwise dig it well in the spring. The better prepared your ground is, the better your herbs will be.

You will need
Digging fork
Small fork (same size as trowel)
Seedlings
Box
Trowel
Watering can
Potted plants
Well-rooted cuttings

Seedlings If your seedlings are in a seed bed, you can move them to an herb bed when they're about 10cm tall.
1. Prepare the ground (see p. 20).

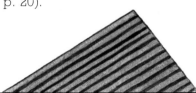

2. With a small fork, carefully dig up the seedlings from your seed bed. Leave some soil on the roots.

---

3. Lay them in a box to take them to the herb bed. Keep them shaded, as hot sun will make them wilt.

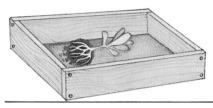

4. With a trowel, dig one hole in the herb bed for each seedling. Leave space for them to spread out.

5. Fill the holes with water.

6. Put the seedlings into the holes.

7. Fill in around the seedlings with soil. Firm well, using your knuckles.

8. If the bed gets a lot of sun, give your seedlings some shade until they're well-grown. Water regularly.

Plants and cuttings With the trowel, dig one hole in the prepared ground for each plant or cutting. Fill the holes with water.

2. Take the plants out of their pots (see p. 27), unless the pots are fibre that can go into the ground.

3. Be careful not to disturb the roots. Put the plants into the holes. Add soil and firm well. Water.

Sowing seeds indoors

Buy your seeds in early spring from a garden center. You can buy or make seed compost (see below). Sow annuals in March or April. Sow biennials and perennials from May to July. If your herbs are to grow outdoors afterwards in containers or the ground, harden them off first (see p. 3).

You will need
Old cup and 10mm sieve
Coarse sand, peat, garden soil ; or bought seed compost
Seed tray or pot
Piece of wood
Seed packets
Old kitchen fork
Label and sticky tape
Plastic bag and elastic band
Fine-rose watering can

1. Using the cup, mix together one cup of sand and one of peat to every two cups of soil. Sieve mixture.

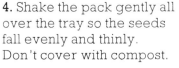

2. Fill the tray up to 2cm from the top with the seed compost mix. Firm it well with the wood. Water well.

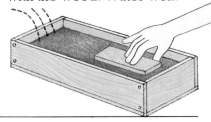

3. If the seeds are very small, mix some dry sand in the seed packet to make it easier to sow the seeds.

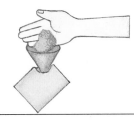

4. Shake the pack gently all over the tray so the seeds fall evenly and thinly. Don't cover with compost.

5. If the seeds are large, make shallow rows in the compost about 2.5cm apart with your finger or a stick.

6. Put the large seeds into the rows at equal spaces from each other.

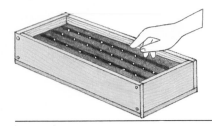

7. Fork compost lightly over the rows of large seeds.

8. Write the name of the herb and the date on a label and tape it to the tray.

9. Carefully put the tray into the bag and seal the end with an elastic band. Put in a warm, dark place.

10. Look at it every day. When seedlings start to grow take off the bag. Put the tray in good indirect light.

11. Water with your fine-rose watering can when dry.

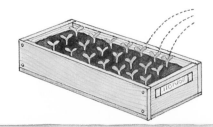

Pricking out

Once your seedlings are big enough to handle, their roots will need more room to grow. Transplant the seedlings from their tray of seed compost to a box of potting compost where they will have more space. This is called 'pricking out'.

You will need
Box or tray
Potting compost from a garden center
Old kitchen fork
Fine-rose watering can

1. When your seedlings are large enough to handle, prick them out into a box of potting compost.

2. Fill the box up to 2cm from the top with potting compost.

3. Make one hole in the compost with a fork.

4. Hold a seedling by a seed leaf (see p.2). Using a fork held in your other hand gently dig from under the roots.

5. Put the seedling into the hole you made in the potting compost. Firm the compost with a finger on each side of the seedling.

6. Dig a hole for another seedling, prick it out, plant it and firm the compost around it. Do this for each seedling. Plant them 4cm apart each way.

7. Water the seedlings well. Then water them regularly and keep the box in good indirect light until the seedlings look strong.

8. Put the box in direct light but give it shade when the sun is very strong. Keep the compost moist but not too wet.

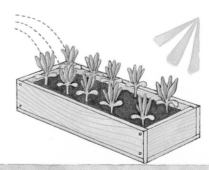

Propagating

It's exciting to take cuttings and watch them grow into new plants. It's a good way to multiply your plants because it isn't expensive. Take softwood cuttings in spring and early summer and hardwood cuttings in late summer and autumn (see p. 3). You can ask other gardeners for cuttings too.

You will need
Old cup and sharp knife
Peat, coarse sand or bought rooting compost
Rooting powder
Crocks (pieces of broken clay pots)
Pots about 10cm wide
Plants for cuttings
4 sticks
Plastic bag and elastic band
Pots about 9cm wide

1. Using the cup, mix together equal amounts of peat and coarse sand. This mixture is rooting compost.

2. Cover the drainage hole of the pot with a crock so the sharp ends point down.

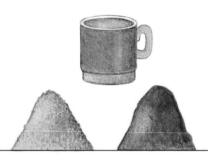

3. Fill the 10cm pot up to 6mm from the top with the rooting compost. Firm it and water well.

4. Ask an adult to cut off the tops of five stems. Each should be firm, not stiff or floppy, 5 to 10cm long and 2 to 3mm thick. Ask for a gardener's help if necessary.

5. Lay the cuttings on a hard surface. **Ask an adult** to cut straight across the stems right below a node (see p.3).

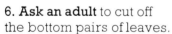

6. Ask an adult to cut off the bottom pairs of leaves.

7. Using a stick, make five holes at equal spaces in the compost against the edge of the pot, deep enough to hold a cutting from its base to its lowest remaining leaves.

8. Dip the end of each cutting into the rooting powder.

Any way that you multiply your plants is called 'propagation'. It isn't easy to take cuttings, but the more you practise the better you will get. Don't be afraid to experiment or ask for advice. Take softwood cuttings of Sage, Rue, Hyssop, Lemon Verbena and Marjoram in spring and summer.

9. Put each cutting into a hole so that its base touches the bottom of a hole. The leaves must not touch each other. Firm the compost with your thumb.

10. Put the sticks into the compost near the edge of the pot at equal distances between the cuttings.

11. Carefully put the pot into a plastic bag. Close the end with an elastic band. Put the pot in a warm place with good indirect light.

12. When you can see that the cuttings are growing (in about four weeks), take off the bag.

13. Turn the pot upside down and tap the rim gently on a table top. The compost will slip out and you will be able to see if the cuttings have grown roots.

14. If you see roots, slide everything back into the pot and leave it for two days without a bag.

15. If you can't see roots, slide everything back into the pot and put the bag back on for another few weeks. Then take out the compost and look for roots again.

16. Put crocks in the bottoms of five 9cm pots. Half-fill the pots with potting compost.

17. Put each cutting into its own pot. Do not plant them deeper than they were before. Firm the compost around them. Water well. Keep them in a sunny place.

You can propagate some plants by taking hardwood cuttings and others by root division. Take hardwood cuttings from Rosemary, Southernwood, Santolina and Lavender in the autumn. You can divide the roots of Mint, Tarragon, Balm, Bergamot, Marjoram, Sorrel and Chives in the spring or autumn.

You will need
Plants to propagate
Sharp knife
Trowel
Coarse sand
Spade
2 garden forks

Hardwood cuttings Ask an adult to cut off a piece of stem about 30 to 40cm long.

2. Take off all the leaves from the bottom half. **Ask an adult** to make a cut straight across the stem just below a node (see p. 3).

3. Using a trowel, dig a hole in the ground next to the plant you took the cuttings from. The hole should be half as deep as the length of your cutting.

4. Put a handful of sand into the hole for good drainage so the tip of the cutting won't rot.

5. Put the cutting into the hole. Add soil around it and firm. Don't water unless very dry. Leave it until late spring, when it will start to grow.

Root division Using a spade, dig up your plant with its roots in the spring before it starts to grow, or in the autumn when it has died down.

2. If you can, divide the plant into two or more clumps by pulling them apart with your hands.

3. If you can't do this, put two forks down into the roots back-to-back. Pull the handles away from each other. Put the new plants into the ground (see p. 21).

Filling containers

Grow Parsley, Sweet Basil, Chives, Thyme, Rosemary, Winter Savory and Variegated Sage in a window box that gets good direct light. Or grow herbs in pots indoors. Grow Basil, Parsley, Chives, Marjoram and Thyme from seeds, Mint from a piece of root and Lemon-scented Geraniums from cuttings.

You will need
Crocks (see p. 24)
Window box on drip tray
Pebbles or small stones
Potting compost
Watering can
Herbs
Scissors
Pots 10 to 13cm wide

Window box Put one crock over each drainage hole so that the sharp ends point down. Put down a thin layer of pebbles or small stones for good drainage.

2. Fill the box up to 5cm from the top with compost, Water well. Put your potted herbs in place on the compost to be sure that you like the arrangement.

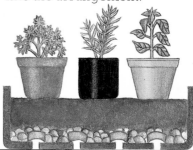

3. Take your herbs out of their pots (see p. 25), unless the pots are fibre that can go into compost. Cut down the sides of polythene pots.

4. Put the herbs on top of the compost where you decided you want them to grow. Be sure they have room to spread out.

5. Using a trowel, carefully add compost around the herbs up to 1.2cm from the top of the box. Try not to disturb the roots. Firm the compost and water.

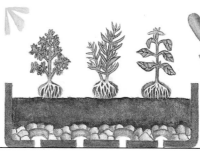
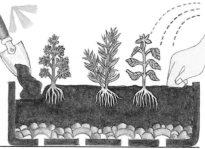

Indoor pots Cover the drainage holes with a crock so that the sharp ends point down.

2. Half fill the pots with potting compost. If your plants are growing in fibre pots, stand them inside a plastic pot.

3. Put your herb on the compost in the pot. Add compost around it up to 2.5cm from the top. Firm well with your knuckles and water.

Drying herbs

Mint, Parsley, Basil, Lemon Balm and Tarragon all keep their full flavors if you dry them in summer to use in winter cooking. You can gather Bay, Rosemary, Sage and Thyme all through the year, but it's a good idea to hang up a spray of each in the kitchen, so they are handy to use in winter.

You will need

Herbs to dry
Scissors
Tray
Pieces of string
Sheets of paper
Sieve
Jars with lids
Sticky labels
Pencil or pen

1. Ask an adult to cut off the top 30 to 45cm of Mint, Balm and Tarragon. Cut herbs before they are in flower. Keep the different herbs separate from each other.

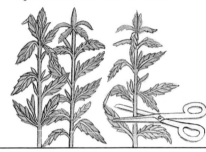

2. Ask an adult to cut off the top 15cm of Parsley and Basil. The best time to cut them is early in the morning after the dew has dried. Put the cut stems on a tray.

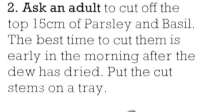

3. Carry them to a shady place. Using string, tie the long stems in bunches, with 12 stems to a bunch. Loop the string so you can pull it tighter as the stems dry.

4. Tie the short stems in bunches with a few stems to a bunch. Loop the string around the bunches the same way as you did for the long stems.

5. Hang all the bunches upside down in a dry place with fresh air. Leave them until the leaves are brittle, in about two or three weeks, tightening the loop.

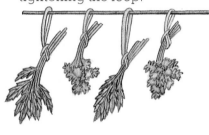

6. Take down one bunch at a time and put it on a sheet of paper. Carefully pick off the leaves. Keep the different herbs on different sheets of paper.

7. Rub the leaves between your hands so that the pieces fall on to a clean sheet of paper. You can rub them through a sieve to make the pieces very fine.

8. Put the pieces into clean jars. Close the lids tightly. Write the herbs and date on labels and stick them to the jars. Store in a cool, dark place till you need them.

Making a lavender bag

You can dry Lavender and then use the flower heads in a pot-pourri (see p. 32) or a sweet-smelling lavender bag. Or you can put the dried Lavender in a vase. Tie a pretty ribbon round the stems after they are dry and stiff.

You will need
Lavender stalks
Scissors
Pieces of string
Paper bag
Sheet of paper
Muslin
Needle and thread
Ribbon

1. Ask an adult to cut off the longest lengths of flower stalks possible. They should be cut just as the bottom row of flowers start to spread their petals.

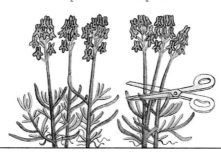

2. Using string, tie the stalks in bunches, with about 20 stalks to a bunch. Loop the string so you can pull it tighter as the stalks dry.

3. Put the stalks into a paper bag, flowers down. Tie a string around the neck of the bag. Hang it in a warm, dry place until the stems are dry and stiff.

4. Take them out of the bag and lay them on a sheet of paper. Hold a stalk in one hand. Rub the flower heads off, using a finger and thumb of your other hand.

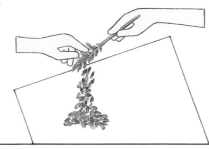

5. Ask an adult to cut out a rectangle-shaped piece of muslin.

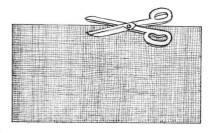

6. Fold it over to double it. With a needle and thread, sew small stitches close to each other along two of the open sides.

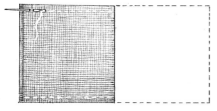

7. Turn the muslin bag inside out. Fill it with the dried pieces of Lavender flower heads.

8. Sew up the open side of the bag. Tie a piece of ribbon in a bow and sew it to the bag.

Making a nosegay

An herb nosegay or 'tussie-mussie' is lovely to make and give to a friend who is ill or who doesn't have a garden. You will need a little practice to become expert at making them. The fun is that each one you make will be different, but they will all smell lovely.

You will need
Herbs
Scissors
Sheet of paper
Piece of string
Jam jar
Silver foil
Ribbon

1. Ask an adult to cut off a few small stems from your herbs that are growing well. Try not to spoil the shapes of your herbs.

2. Be sure you have a flower for the center of your nosegay. Some Lavender stalks, a Marigold, a Rose or Rosemary flowers will look pretty.

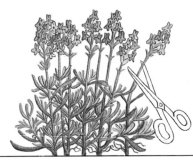

3. Pick Geranium leaves and some sprigs of other herbs. Try to have different shades of green and gray. Put them all on a flat sheet of paper.

4. It's easier to sit down to make your bunch. Start with the flower in the center and arrange your sprigs with small leaves round it.

5. Add your sprigs with larger leaves all round the bunch you are holding. Use Lemon-scented Geranium if you have any. Ivy leaves make a good outside frill.

6. Tie a piece of string round the stalks. It may be easier to **ask an adult** to tie the string while you hold the nosegay. Cut the ends of the stalks.

7. Fill a clean jam jar with water. Put in your nosegay to have a drink.

8. Before you give it away, wrap some silver foil around the stems or tie a colorful ribbon around it to hide the string.

Making a pomander

People in the 16th century used pomanders and scented balls to protect themselves from diseases and nasty smells. It is easy to make orange and clove pomanders to hang up in your wardrobe or kitchen. Pomanders are good Christmas presents to make for friends and family.

You will need
Large orange
Knitting needle
Cloves
Cinnamon and orris root powder
Tablespoon
Sheet of paper
Silver foil
Long piece of ribbon

1. Using the knitting needle, carefully punch holes at equal spaces all over the outer skin of the orange.

2. Push the stem of a clove into a hole.

3. Fill all the holes with cloves in this way.

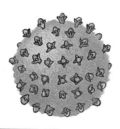

4. If you can get cinnamon and orris root, mix together equal amounts to make one tablespoon. Your pomander will smell much nicer.

5. Spread the mixture on a clean sheet of paper. Roll the orange to and fro in the mixture. Be sure it gets between the cloves.

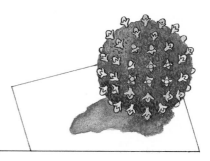

6. Wrap silver foil around the orange. Put it in a dry place for about three or four weeks. The orange will get smaller as it dries.

7. Take off the foil. Wrap a long piece of ribbon once or twice around the orange laying it between the cloves.

8. Tie the ribbon firmly. Make a neat bow, or leave enough ribbon for a loop so that you can hang up your pomander.

Making a pot-pourri

This is the 'moist' way to make a pot-pourri. It's the best way because the perfume gets stronger after a year instead of fading. You must put in Rose petals, which form the base of the pot-pourri. You also have to add Lavender flowers because they have oil in them which keeps pot-pourri moist.

You will need
Roses, Lavender flowers and other herbs
Clippers
Tray
Sheet of paper
Old cup and tablespoon
Salt
½-kilo jars and lids
Orris root powder
Bowls
Plastic bag and ribbon

1. Ask an adult to cut off Rose stalks in June and July. The flowers should be open but not fading. Be careful of the thorns.

2. Carry the flowers indoors. Carefully take off the petals, and lay them on a sheet of paper. If you can see any insects on the petals take them off.

3. Spread out the petals on a tray. They should be in a warm place with fresh air, but not in a draft. Let them dry for one day, when they will feel leathery.

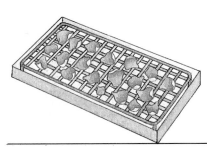

4. Using a cup, measure out the petals. For every two cups of petals, measure ¼ cup of salt. Mix them together. The salt stops the petals from getting brittle.

5. Put the mixture into a clean jar. Close the lid tightly.

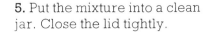

6. Shake gently. Leave the jar for two weeks, shaking it gently every other day.

7. At the end of two weeks, shake a little orris root powder into the jar. It helps to keep the scent.

8. During those two weeks, get the rest of your pot-pourri ready. **Ask an adult** to cut off the stalks of any herbs that have scented leaves. Carry them indoors.

The old-fashioned Roses, such as the Gallicas and Rugosas, are the best to use in your pot-pourri because they keep their scents when dry. Modern Tea Roses and Floribundas lose their perfume. **Ask an adult** if you're not sure which kinds to add. You can plant your own Roses in your herb garden.

9. Take off the leaves. Lay them on a tray. Keep each kind separate. Let them dry for three or four days.

10. Put each kind of leaf into its own clean ½-kilo jar. Add one tablespoon of salt to each full jar. Close the lids tightly.

11. Shake the jars to mix the salt with the leaves. Put them aside until you need them.

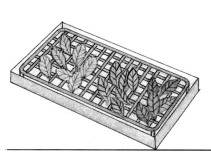

12. Gather and dry Lavender flowers (see p. 29).

13. Mix Rose petals and Lavender flowers in a few bowls. To each bowl, add a few handfuls of the differently-scented leaves.

14. Put the mixtures into jars. Close the lids tightly. Leave them for six weeks. Stir from time to time with a spoon.

15. If the mixture seems very dry when you stir, add some salt.

16. Put your pot-pourris into pretty bowls. Or put them into plastic bags and tie the ends closed with ribbons, ready to give away.

Making tea

The word *tisane* is French. It means herbal tea. Pronounce it "tee-zahn". You can make *tisanes* with leaves of Mint, Marjoram, Thyme, Rosemary, Sage, Balm, Parsley or Bergamot, or flowers of Bergamot or Chamomile. You can also use fruits, or rose hips, of Rugosa Roses in autumn. **Don't make tea from any other leaves or flowers.** Use a handful of fresh leaves or two teaspoonfuls of dried leaves or flowers for every half-liter of water.

You will need
Leaves or flowers
Sharp knife
Kettle
China teapot
Tea cups
Teaspoon
Honey, sugar or lemon
Strainer
Clean jar

1. Gather your herbs. **Ask an adult** to chop them into small pieces.

2. **Ask an adult** to boil at least a half-liter of water in a kettle.

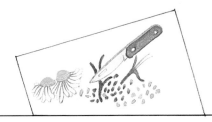

3. While you are waiting for the water to boil, warm a china teapot. Put in a handful of chopped herbs.

4. **Ask an adult** to pour the boiling water into the teapot.

5. Put on the lid. Let it brew for five minutes to get the full flavor and keep in the aroma.

6. Pour out the tea into cups. Add spoonfuls of honey or sugar, or squeeze in a few drops of lemon juice.

7. If there is any tea left in the pot, pour it through a strainer into a clean jar. You can heat it up later.

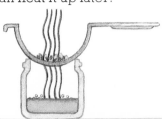

Tea made by boiling rose hips in water is called a 'decoction'. Have this as a cold drink. The best kind of rose hips, or fruits, to use grow on Rugosa Roses. If you don't have any, ask a gardener who does if you can pick some. Be sure that you gather them in the autumn, before the birds eat them!

You will need
Sharp scissors
Rose hips
Tray
Clean jug or bottle
Enamel saucepan
Strainer
Tea cup
Teaspoon
Honey
Bowl

1. Ask an adult to cut off the rose hips of Rugosa Roses in the autumn.

2. Rub off all their whiskers. **Ask an adult** to cut off the stems. Wash the rose hips.

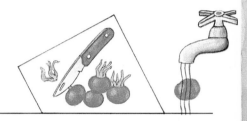

3. Put the hips into an enamel saucepan. Add enough water to cover them.

4. Ask an adult to put the pan on a stove. Bring it to the boil and simmer for 15 minutes.

5. Ask an adult to take the pan off the heat. Let the liquid cool.

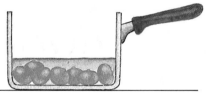

6. Pour the liquid through a strainer into a tea cup.

7. Add a teaspoonful of honey.

8. If there is any decoction left, pour it through a strainer into a clean jug or bottle to drink later.

9. You can dry rose hips to use later. Put them on a tray in a warm, dark place until they feel dry.

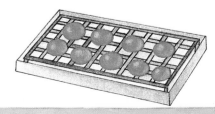

10. Put them in a clean jar. Close the lid tightly.

11. The day before you use them, soak them in water in a bowl.

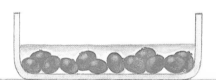

Helpful hints

These suggestions will help you grow healthy herbs and keep them healthy.

Clipping hard or pruning
This means cutting your shrubby herbs (see p. 3) with scissors or clippers so that you take off growth that is a year or less old. Then new shoots will grow into a neat, firm bush. If you cut into the older wood, new shoots may not grow.

Clip or prune all your gray shrubs in the spring.

Cut the perennials Mint, Balm, Tarragon, Bergamot, Marjoram, Fennel, Sorrel, Lovage, Sweet Chervil and Chives right down to the ground in autumn.

Prune Sage, Winter Savory, Bay, Hyssop, Rue, Lavender, Roses, Santolina, Rosemary, Southernwood and Thyme in spring.

Compost heap
You can make a compost heap by putting kitchen waste such as old vegetable matter, fruit skins and tea bags and garden waste such as weeds, dead leaves and lawn mowings into a bin and letting it rot. You can buy a special bin or **ask an adult** to help you make your own.

Drive four stakes, each 1.2m long, into the ground one-half to 1m apart, so that they form a square. Using a hammer, nail old wooden planks across the stakes to make a bin. You can use wire netting if you can't get old planks.

Put your kitchen and garden waste into the bin. You can even use small amounts of soaked and shredded newspaper. Spread everything in layers in your bin.

You will have to buy a special compost maker at a garden center. This helps to break down the waste matter. Follow the directions on the packet.

The waste matter will heat up and then break down into good compost. This takes three to four months in the summer and longer in the winter. When the compost is ready, you can mix it with peat and use it in containers, or spread it over your herb bed.

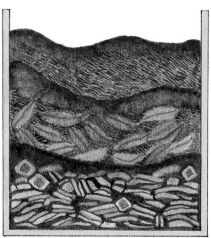

Feeding
You need to eat food with vitamins and minerals to be strong and healthy. Your plants need good food too. Potting compost that you buy has all the things in it that your plants need, but these get used up in three or four months, so feed your herbs with a fertilizer from a garden center.

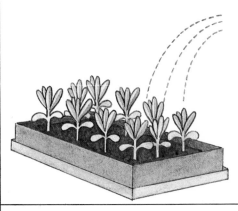

Never be frightened to ask advice from good gardeners. They like to pass on their knowledge.

Plants to grow from seed each spring: Parsley, Basil, Borage, Nasturtium, Marigold and Summer Savory.

Biennials to grow from seed from June to August: Angelica and Woad.

Plants to keep indoors in the winter: Lemon-scented Geranium.

Thinning out

This means pulling out some seedlings from where they are growing, so that the ones you leave have more space to grow. In pots and trays, thin out so the seedlings left are 3 to 5cm apart. In a seed bed, thin out to 5 to 7cm apart.

Go to seed

This means not cutting off flowers when they die. The flowers will make seeds which ripen and fall to the ground nearby. New seedlings, called self-sown seedlings, will grow around the parent plant. You can collect ripe seeds and sow these yourself.

Hints for planting:

1. Dig a hole that is large enough for the roots to grow without being crowded.
2. Fill the hole with water before you put in your plant.
3. Be sure the herb is planted firmly. Gently try to pull it out – if it will come out, firm around it again.
4. Remember to water your plants and to inspect them for slugs.

Most herbs like a well-drained soil. This is soil which lets water run through it quite easily, so that the roots of your herbs won't be growing in sticky soil. Clay soil is badly drained. A gravelly, sandy soil is well-drained.

To get Chives or Parsley a bit earlier than usual, put a one-kilo jam jar over your plant. This keeps it warm.

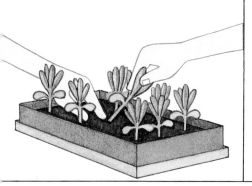

Pests and diseases

Herbs get very few pests and diseases. Instead, they tend to keep away the pests.

Black fly and green fly These pests are often attracted to the young flowering shoots of Lovage and Borage. Use a spray from a garden center to kill them.

Slugs and snails These pests eat the young leaves of herbs. Put half a pineapple skin on the ground with the fleshy side down. Slugs will gather inside at night and you can kill them in the morning.

Plant chart

Name and type	Height	How to propagate	Light
Angelica HB	1.5m	SD out	sun or shade
Anise HA	30–60cm	SD in or out	sun
Basil HHA	30–40cm	SD in or out	sun
Bay S	up to 3m	HC	sun
Bergamot HP	70cm–1m	RD	sun
Borage A and B	50cm–1m	SD in or out	sun
Caraway HB	30–40cm	SD in or out	sun
Chamomile EP	10–30cm	SD ; RD	sun
Chives HP	15–30cm	SD ; RD	sun
Cress HA	5–10cm	SD in	see p.7
Dill HHA	40–60cm	SD in or out	sun
Fennel HP	1m	SD out	sun or shade
Garlic HP	30–40cm	SD in or out ; cloves	sun
Geranium HHS	50cm–1m	SC	sun
Goose Foot HP	30–40cm	SD in or out ; RD	sun or shade
Hyssop HS	50–60cm	SD in or out ; SC	sun
Lavender HS	35–60cm	SD in or out ; HC	sun
Lemon Balm HP	40–60cm	RD	sun
Lemon Verbena HHS	1–2m	SC	sun
Lovage HP	1–1.5m	SD out	sun
Marigold HA	30–40cm	SD in or out	sun
Marjoram HP	30–40cm	SD in or out ; RD	sun
Mint HP	50–70cm	SD in or out ; RD	sun or shade
Parsley HB grow as HA	30–45cm	SD in or out	sun or shade
Rosemary HS	60cm–1m	SD in or out ; SC ; HC	sun or shade
Rue HS	40–60cm	SD in or out ; SC	sun or shade
Sage, Gray HS	70cm	SD in or out ; SC	sun or shade
Sage, Purple HS	70cm	SD in or out ; SC	sun or shade
Sage, Tri-color HS	40cm	SC	sun or shade
Santolina HS	30–60cm	SC	sun
Savory, Summer HA	30cm	SD in or out	sun or shade
Savory, Winter EP	30cm	SD in or out ; SC	sun or shade
Sorrel HP	20–40cm	SD in or out ; RD	sun or shade
Southernwood HS	30–60cm	SC ; HC	sun or shade
Sweet Chervil HP	70–90cm	SD in or out	light shade
Tarragon HP	40–60cm	RD	sun
Thyme EP	10–40cm	RC ; SC	sun
Tree Onion HP	50–60cm	Bulbs	sun
Woad HB	1m	SD in or out	sun or shade

Key to abbreviations

HA – Hardy Annual	HHS – Half-Hardy Shrub
HHA – Half-Hardy Annual	SD – Seed
HB – Hardy Biennial	SD in or out – seeds can be sown indoors in trays or outdoors into ground
HP – Hardy Perennial	SC – Softwood Cuttings
EP – Evergreen Perennial	HC – Hardwood Cuttings
HS – Hardy Shrub	RD – Root Division

Grow in containers	When to harvest	Use	Part to use
no	summer-autumn	cooking	stem
no	autumn	cooking	seeds
yes	summer-autumn	cooking	leaf
yes	all year	cooking	leaf
no	just before flowering	tea; pot-pourri	flower; leaf
no	summer	cooking	flower; leaf
no	autumn	cooking	seeds
yes	all year	tea; pot-pourri	flower; leaf
yes	all year	cooking	leaf
yes	all year	cooking	leaf
no	summer-autumn	cooking	leaf; seeds
no	summer-autumn	cooking	leaf
yes	all year	cooking	cloves
yes	all year	cooking	leaf
no	spring-summer	cooking	leaf; young shoots
yes	spring-autumn	cooking	leaf
yes	summer-autumn	pot-pourri; bag	leaf; flowers
no	spring-autumn	tea; pot-pourri	leaf
yes	summer-autumn	pot-pourri; cooking	leaf
no	summer-autumn	cooking	leaf
yes	summer-autumn	pot-pourri; cooking	flowers
yes	spring-autumn	cooking	leaf
yes	spring-autumn	cooking	leaf
yes	spring-autumn	cooking	leaf
yes	all year	pot-pourri; cooking	leaf; flowers
yes	spring-autumn	pot-pourri	leaf
yes	all year	pot-pourri; cooking	leaf
yes	all year	pot-pourri; cooking	leaf
yes	all year	pot-pourri	leaf
no	summer	pot-pourri	leaf
yes	summer	pot-pourri; cooking	leaf; flowers
yes	autumn-winter	pot-pourri; cooking	leaf; flowers
no	summer	cooking	leaf
yes	summer	pot-pourri	leaf
no	summer	pot-pourri; cooking	leaf; seeds
yes	summer	cooking	leaf
yes	all year	cooking	leaf
no	summer	cooking	top bulb
no	summer	dyeing	leaf

Index

Latin names are in *italic*.
Page numbers in *italic* refer to illustrations.

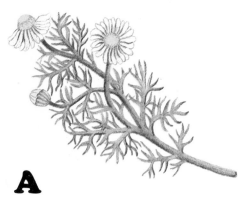